REACHING THE NEXT GENERATION

Strategies for Evangelizing Today's Youth

Mel Walker

REGULAR BAPTIST PRESS
1300 North Meacham Road
Schaumburg, Illinois 60173-4806

This publication mentions Web sites that provide information useful for a specific purpose. Regular Baptist Press is not responsible for the contents of any off-site Web page referenced in this publication. Reference in this publication to any outside Web site, product, process, service, or company does not constitute its endorsement or recommendation by Regular Baptist Press.

REACHING THE NEXT GENERATION:
STRATEGIES FOR EVANGELIZING TODAY'S YOUTH
© 2004
Regular Baptist Press • Schaumburg, Illinois
1-800-727-4440
www.regularbaptistspress.org • www.rbpstudentministries.org
Printed in U.S.A.
All rights reserved
RBP5321 • ISBN: 0-87227-415-2

Contents

Introduction 7

CHAPTER 1 Why Reach Teenagers? 11

CHAPTER 2 The History of Youth Ministry in a Context of Evangelistic Movements 23

CHAPTER 3 Determining Your Youth Evangelism Strategy 31

               Lifestyle Evangelism 32

               Event Evangelism 41

               Public School Outreach 54

               Door-to-Door or Visitation Evangelism 59

CHAPTER 4 Outreach Ideas 67

Conclusion 75

Addendum 79

Selected Bibliography 83

Dedication

This book is dedicated to *Miss Rosemary Clark,* a missionary with Child Evangelism Fellowship who ministered in my home town, and to *all the children's and youth workers at my home church, Bridgewater Baptist Church of Montrose, Pennsylvania.*

Miss Clark loved children and young people, and she longed to reach them for Jesus Christ. She shared the gospel with me when I was five years old.

I also want to share my deepest thanks to all of my childhood Sunday School teachers and youth workers at Bridgewater for putting up with me and ministering to me during my formative and growing years. Their impact for Christ continues to this day in my life as I attempt to challenge other churches and youth workers to reach students for Christ.

Acknowledgments

I want to express my thanks to four groups of people.

My wife and family. First of all, I sincerely thank my wife, Peggy, and our three kids for their support of this project. My wife has taught me much about the subject of evangelism. Her boldness in sharing her faith has been an example to me. I also want to say thanks to Kristi, Todd, and Travis for their love for people and their commitment to share the gospel.

The youth workers who participated in my survey. Next, I want to thank the four-hundred-plus youth workers who participated in my survey on evangelism. I am thankful their input and ideas. I was encouraged to see so many youth workers who are burdened to reach the next generation for Christ.

The youth group at Heritage Baptist Church. I also want to express my thanks to the members of the student ministry at Heritage Baptist Church of Clarks Summit, Pennsylvania. I have been blessed to hear their testimonies of opportunities they have had to witness for Christ. It is exciting to see students with a burden for their unsaved friends.

The production staff at Regular Baptist Press. Finally, I want to say a heart-felt thank you to the editorial and graphics departments at Regular Baptist Press. You are dear friends, and I appreciate your hard work to make writers look good in print. Thank you.

Introduction

TODAY'S TEENAGERS may be more open to the gospel than at any other time in modern history.

I can certainly vouch for the validity of that statement in my lifetime. I have been actively involved in youth ministry for almost thirty years. I witnessed the Jesus people/coffeehouse movement of the 1960s. I ministered during the "bus-'em-in" craze of the '70s. I watched the anti-humanism, pro-Christian-school emphasis of the '80s. I appreciated the push in the '90s to reach out to public schools through on-campus Bible clubs and prayer rallies. Now I am seeing the emphasis upon religion and spiritual things in this new millennium.

I have not only seen these trends take place, but I have also taught youth ministry classes on college and seminary levels for more than twenty years. I have studied the historic and visionary youth rallies, which were led by men such as Percy Crawford and Jack Wyrtzen in the 1940s, and the rise of youth and children's clubs, such as Young Life and Awana, in the '50s.

I have also traveled around the United States

enough to observe how churches use youth ministry programs such as Word of Life and Pro-Teens to reach teens for Christ and to build Christian kids in their faith. I have served as a youth pastor in a local church, and I have worked with numerous other churches in the calling and hiring of their youth pastors. A few years ago I helped start a youth ministry organization that exists to train youth workers. I have also served as a youth speaker at numerous youth conferences, camps, retreats, and rallies. In addition to my role as a developer and writer of youth ministry curriculum and other resources at Regular Baptist Press, my wife and I currently serve as youth workers in our home church, and I help lead a small group of senior high guys. I am also actively involved in mentoring and discipling others.

I relate all of this information to emphasize that even though the last several decades have featured many ways to reach young people with the gospel, we may now be living in the most wide-open time in history to reach teenagers for Christ.

Even though I work hard to study youth ministry history and to observe youth ministry trends, I cannot predict with certainty what the next emphasis to reach teenagers for Christ will be. Unquestionably the new millennium has brought a great deal of interest in worship and music. Concerts and praise festivals abound. Something along those lines may ultimately be the next great youth ministry trend. Sports certainly have a vice grip on our culture; churches may realize that athletics can somehow be the next wave of youth ministry outreach. Mentoring is also a current hot topic. This adult-teen connection may be the way to reach Millennial kids for Christ. (For additional thoughts on the subject of mentoring, see my book *Mentoring the Next Generation: A Strategy for Connecting the Generations,* published by Regular Baptist Press.) I also agree with contemporary writers such as Josh McDowell and Ravi Zacharias, who believe that "relational apologetics" may be the tool that God will use for personal evangelism in our postmodern culture.[1]

Today's church needs a wake-up call for youth evangelism. We cannot rely on the trends or methods of the past, and we dare not relegate our responsibility to reach students for Christ to parachurch ministries or professional youth ministry organizations. The church's mandate is to evangelize the lost; it is "crunch time" for the church to develop and initiate creative and culturally effective means to reach today's teenagers with the gospel.

NOTES
1. For more information, visit www.gospelcom.net/rzim and www.josh.org.

CHAPTER 1

Why Reach Teenagers?

God may be giving us the greatest opportunity we have ever had to see teenagers come to Christ. Today's students are open to the message of the gospel. God is at work in the lives of this generation, and the church has an open door to reach teenagers for Christ.

Here are seven reasons why I believe our churches must make youth evangelism a top priority in this millennium.

today's students are open to the message of the gospel.

1. Teenagers are a large and needy mission field. The year 2000 brought a cultural shift that is having an incredible impact around the world. That shift is the rise of the Millennials, or the Millennial Generation, which I define as those who graduated from high school during or after the year 2000. According to researchers Neil Howe and William Strauss, "Already America has well over 80 million Millennials. By the time future immigrants join their U.S.-born peers, this generation will probably top 100 million members, making it nearly a third bigger than the Boomers."[1]

"Yes, millennials are numerous. Swelled by a resurgent fertility rate and by the large families of a record immigration surge, they indeed are a giant of a generation."[2] The sheer size of this generation cannot truly be grasped until we realize that "well over one third of all the people in the world are teenagers or younger."[3]

> We have more teenagers now than we have had for several years.

The magnitude of Millennials means that today's teenagers will continue to have a huge impact upon society for years to come. The Millennial Generation will present ample opportunities for churches to reach out into their communities via youth ministry. The fact that we have more teenagers now than we have had for several years should provide multiple open doors for evangelism.

Another reason for reaching out to the Millennial Generation is that many of today's teenagers have tremendous needs. Sin is rampant. Youth are struggling with moral purity and sexual issues, substance abuse, parental and family crises, violence, and numerous other challenges.

Being a teenager today is difficult. But believers in

Christ have hope. Remember that in the darkness of this society, the light of Christ can shine brightly. We must teach Christian students to stand up for the Lord, and we must teach them how to share their faith in Christ with others.

American teenagers are a large and needy mission field, and it is important that we look at them that way. Effective ministry to teenagers is a cross-cultural experience. Our churches need to develop creative, culturally relevant yet Biblically based youth ministries to reach this large generation for Christ.

> **The vast majority of people accept Christ as Savior before they reach the age of eighteen.**

2. *Most people accept Christ before the age of eighteen.* Another reason why churches must make youth evangelism a top priority is because the vast majority of people accept Christ as Savior before they reach the age of eighteen. According to the Barna Research Group, six out of ten people make their decision to accept Christ before age eighteen.[4] However, a survey by Dave Rahn and Terry Linhart, the authors of *Contagious Faith,* indicates that almost 92 percent of Christian adults accepted Christ before they turned eighteen.[5]

In preparing for this book, I surveyed more than four hundred youth workers in a variety of conferences and seminars around the country. My quick, albeit unscientific, survey revealed that close to 85 percent of today's youth workers accepted Christ before they became adults. Rahn and Linhart substantiate this statistic by concluding that "many veterans in ministry would agree that the teenage years are when a significant number of conversions to Christianity take place."[6]

3. *Today's teenagers are open to religion and spiritual things.* Churches should make youth outreach a priority because today's students are interested in religion, and they are open to spiritual things. In his book *The Bridger Generation,* Thom Rainer made this statement: "History may remember the bridger generation [Rainer's term for the Millennials] as the most religious group America has ever known. Their generation is being raised in a time when the Gallup Organization reports that religion is playing a more important role in the lives of Americans.... Church attendance has held steady for most age groups, but is increasing among the bridger generation."[7]

Brief samplings of current media show a religious resurgence in modern culture. One prime-time television lineup contained a program geared for teenagers about a student who has a personal relationship with God. Religious books have dominated best-seller lists. Movies with religious or spiritual themes (for example, *The Lord of the Rings,* the Harry Potter movies, and *The*

Passion of the Christ) are often the most popular among teens and preteens, and countless news reports show that young people from all over the world detonate suicide bombs under the guise of religious fanaticism. One church growth consultant mused that today's Millennials may be the first generation since America's founding fathers to consider religion and involvement in church to be culturally acceptable or cool.

If these cultural indicators are indeed true, then we have an incredible opportunity to encourage and motivate Christian students to be bold in their endeavors to witness to their friends and to invite their unsaved friends to church and church-related outreach events. This openness to spiritual things gives your Christian students unparalleled opportunities to share their faith with others. We should work hard to make sure our students know how to share the gospel with their friends, coworkers, family members, neighbors, and classmates. (See chapter 3 for more information.)

> Encourage and motivate Christian students to be bold in their endeavors to witness.

4. *Reaching young people now means that you can impact the future.* I have often stated that the most important reason for reaching teenagers is that they will grow up someday. Many of my colleagues in youth ministry have said that youth aren't just the church of tomorrow; they are part of the church today.

I certainly believe that statement is true. However, it is imperative for our churches to invest in Millennials because we are investing in our future. History is lined with the stories of churches and religious movements that became weak and ineffective because they did not make reaching young people a top priority. If we fail to reach the next generation, our churches will face an aging membership that will ultimately pass away. That is why it is critically important for today's churches to protect their future by strategically reaching out to Millennials.

> It is critically important for today's churches to protect their future by stategically reaching out to Millennials.

By the end of this decade, the Millennial Generation will be moving through high school, out of college, and into the work force. They will be making adult decisions in a world that will be dominated by their peers. It is critical that we invest in the future and reach this generation now.

5. *A strong youth ministry can reach parents and families.* Another reason for making youth evangelism a top priority is that teenagers have the ability to reach their parents and other family members for Christ. I know of several instances where this scenario has happened. Students who have come to Christ through various means of local church outreach have been bur-

dened to follow up their decision by telling their loved ones about their newfound faith. Not too long ago I had the opportunity to lead two young people to Christ at a youth rally in the Midwest. In the first few months following their conversion, both students shared their faith with unsaved family members. And both of them had the great privilege of seeing those family members come to Christ. A few months earlier, I had spoken at a youth conference on the West Coast. That weekend several teenagers came to know Christ as their Savior. I have received word that one of those students had the opportunity to lead both his parents to Christ.

> **Teenagers have the ability to reach their parents and other family members for Christ.**

6. *Many spiritual revivals have started with students.* "At the turn of the twentieth century, American psychologist Edwin Starbuck concluded, 'This much we can say with certainty, that spontaneous awakenings are distinctly adolescent phenomena.' "[8]

God has used students in unique ways as catalysts for spiritual revivals. These events occurred during great historical movements, such as the Great Awakening, but they also continue to take place in smaller ways in churches around the country. A multitude of reasons contribute to these events, but I think that teenagers' idealistic outlook on life gives them the confidence that God can indeed use them to accomplish something great for Him.

A modern example of an adolescent revival may be the student-led national prayer movement, See You at the Pole. In early 1990, a youth group from Burleson, Texas, returned from a weekend youth conference with a burden for the public high schools in their community. They met the next week at the school's flagpole to pray specifically for friends and the school. Within a few weeks, the story of this youth group's burden spread throughout Texas and to other surrounding states. By September 2001, almost one million teenagers from around the country were meeting at their schools' flagpoles for a time of prayer and worship—and a movement was born. In 2003, more than four million high school students met for See You at the Pole on the third Wednesday of September.[9]

> God has used students in unique ways as catalysts for spiritual revivals.

It may not be a genuine revival, but God has a way of using youth to bring life and energy into stale environments. I witnessed such a revival when I was a youth pastor in Michigan. God used a small number of our students to impact the whole church. After the students made personal and public commitments to Christ, their overwhelming desires were to live for Him and to tell others about Him. Some of the students started Bible studies and prayer groups in their public schools. Soon several adults followed the lead of the students and made public commitments to live for Christ. Over a period of several months we saw God do some great things in our youth group and church as more and more students made commitments to follow Christ.

> **God has a way of using youth to bring life and energy into stale environments.**

Undoubtedly other youth workers could share their own stories of how the Lord has used students to impact entire churches for evangelistic outreach. I have also had many opportunities over the years to hear how God has used teenagers who made decisions or commitments at camps or conferences to influence the adults in their churches back home. Youth evangelism must be emphasized because of its potential for spiritual revival throughout the whole church.

7. *The Bible gives a mandate of evangelism.* Of all the reasons why it is essential to reach teenagers for Christ, the most significant reason is that God has given us a mandate to share the gospel. The Lord Jesus Christ gave this New Testament directive in the Great Commission: "Go ye therefore, and teach all nations, baptizing them in the name of the Father, and of the Son, and of the Holy Ghost: teaching them to observe all things whatsoever I have commanded you: and, lo, I

am with you alway, even unto the end of the world" (Matt. 28:19, 20). The imperative in this passage, of course, is to make disciples. However, the text assumes that "Go" is understood. In other words, Christ's Great Commission could be stated this way, "As you are going, make disciples." Christ's last words to His followers gave them the marching orders for outreach and evangelism.

> God has given us a mandate to share the gospel.

This mind-set continues in Acts 1:8: "But ye shall receive power, after that the Holy Ghost is come upon you: and ye shall be witnesses unto me both in Jerusalem, and in all Judaea, and in Samaria, and unto the uttermost part of the earth." Again we have a basic assumption. Christ did not tell His followers to go out witnessing. He told them that they would be witnesses. Witnessing would happen naturally as they went about their day-to-day responsibilities of living for the Lord. Being a witness for Christ was assumed.

The apostle Paul's letters to the first-century churches contain passages, such as 2 Corinthians 5:18–20, which demonstrate that evangelism is a major priority for all believers. God in Christ "committed unto us the word of reconciliation." We are "ambassadors for Christ."

The responsibility for outreach was given to church leaders in the Pastoral Epistles. Second Timothy 4:5 instructs young church leaders to "do the work of an evangelist." Certainly the great task of outreach requires diligence and hard work.

The apostle Peter also spoke of the believer's responsibility for outreach in 1 Peter 3:15: "Be ready always to give an answer to every man that asketh you a reason of the hope that is in you with meekness and fear."

These verses are just a sampling of the Biblical priority of outreach and evangelism. But another priority in Scripture also relates to this subject. I am referring to what I call the "Next Generation Principle." (For additional comments on this topic, see my book on youth discipleship, *Impacting the Next Generation: A Strategy for Discipleship in Youth Ministry*.) God's Word gives numerous examples of His people who made "spiritual reproduction" in the lives of the next generation a priority. Examples include Moses and Joshua, Elijah and Elisha, Barnabas and John Mark, Paul and Timothy, even Christ and His disciples. These individuals substantiate the importance of reaching the next generation.

> One of the most important priorities for any church, or fellowship of churches for that matter, is to impact the next generation.

I earnestly believe that one of the most important priorities for any church, or fellowship of churches for that matter, is to impact the next generation. It is the very nature of what the Lord left His followers here on earth to do. We must make youth evangelism a top priority in this new millennium. God has given us a great opportunity to reach this generation for eternity. I believe we need this wake-up call. Churches need a call to action. It's time to get going. It's time to reach students for Christ.

NOTES

1. Neil Howe and William Strauss, *Millennials Go to College* (Great Falls, Va.: American Association of Collegiate Registrars, 2003), 35.

2. Neil Howe and William Strauss, *Millennials Rising: The Next Great Generation* (New York, Random House, Vintage Books), 14.

3. Dave Rahn and Terry Linhart, *Contagious Faith: Empowering Student Leadership in Youth Evangelism* (Loveland, Colo.: Group Publishing, 2000), 18.

4. See www.barna.org/cgi-bin/MainArchives.asp.

5. See www.groupmag.com/articles/details.asp?ID=3987.

6. Rahn and Linhart, 19.

7. Thom S. Rainer, *The Bridger Generation* (Nashville: Broadman & Holman Publishers, 1997), 151.

8. Edwin D. Starbuck, *The Psychology of Religion: An Empirical Study of the Growth of Religious Consciousness;* quoted by Dean Borgman in "A History of American Youth Ministry," chap. 4 of *The Complete Book of Youth Ministry,* Warren S. Benson and Mark H. Senter III, eds. (Chicago: Moody Press, 1987), 62.

9. Visit www.syatp.com/Info/History.html for a brief history of the See You at the Pole movement.

CHAPTER 2

The History of Youth Ministry in a Context of Evangelistic Movements

The history of youth ministry is a veritable "who's who" of dedicated and visionary individuals who creatively and confidently communicated the gospel to teenagers. Ever since the dawning of the youth culture in western civilization, the Lord has used imaginative leaders who were burdened to reach into that culture in an attempt to reach students for Christ.

The Lord has used imaginative leaders who were burdened to reach into that culture in an attempt to reach students for Christ.

Today's youth workers would do well to study history's evangelistic trends in youth ministry to see how God has used different means and methodologies in various periods and cultures to impact teenagers for eternity.

Several years ago Dean Borgman contributed a chapter on the history of youth ministry in *The Complete Book of Youth Ministry.* He made this astute observation: "History should never be a mere chronicle of events. . . . History, especially a history of youth ministry, should describe the spirit of the times and its cultures, and it should depict visions and trends. From history we need inspiration, a few lessons, and encouragement."[1]

Since its inception, youth ministry has been the story of visionary leaders who were used by the Lord to identify trends and needs in contemporary culture and who were burdened to develop creative ways to meet those needs by effectively sharing the gospel of Christ to students. By its very nature, youth ministry is a need-based phenomenon. People and churches saw that young people had definite needs, so they purposed to design ministries to meet those needs.

Perhaps classic youth ministry finds its roots in historical and legendary movements such as the Sunday School. The idea of a Sunday School originated with Robert Raikes in England in 1780. Raikes had a burden to provide needy children with the opportunity to learn the Bible. The genius of his strategy was really quite simple: he saw kids with needs, and he organized a ministry to meet those needs. The Sunday School gave children and youth something to do, and it provided a way to effectively and creatively communicate God's Word.

Modern youth ministry can be traced to America in the 1940s and to visionary leaders such as Percy Crawford and Jack Wyrtzen. The Lord used these men, and others of that era, to organize what were to become the first youth rallies. Their idea was that members of this country's emerging youth culture would be attracted to the music of their generation and to the preaching of God's Word from effective youth communicators. Their approach was simple—lively music and a youth speaker—yet they set the trend in youth ministry for years and years to come.

The 1940s also saw the rise of the youth group or youth club concept and the formation of organizations such as Young Life and Youth For Christ.[2] These ministries came into existence to give teenagers a place to meet with other young people, and a warm, encouraging environment for their leaders to teach God's Word.

The next cycle of youth ministry saw the emergence of organizations such as Christian Service Brigade (established by Joseph Coughlin in 1937) and

Awana (spearheaded by Lance Latham and Art Rorheim in 1950). These programs used a military motif of uniforms and badges, effectively utilized by the Boy Scouts, to reach out to the post-World War II youth culture.[3]

The 1960s have become synonymous with American youth culture. It was the decade of the Beatles, Woodstock, hippies, and riots in U.S. cities. Many wise and visionary youth leaders saw this time period as the perfect opportunity to reach out this country's booming youth population. This vision was the idea behind Campus Life, the Fellowship of Christian Athletes, and other youth ministry organizations that began during the '60s.[4]

In *The Coming Revolution,* Mark Senter made the following statement: "During the years between the middle of the 1950s and the end of the 1960s, the position of 'youth pastor' became established as an important part of a pastoral staff in evangelical churches. . . . The youth pastor was a response to the vocal presence of middle class adolescents as factors in the American way of life. So compelling was the teenage generation that, had Young Life and Youth for Christ not been present, youth pastors would have appeared on the scene anyway"[5]

The 1970s brought a growing legitimacy to vocational youth ministry. Led by Christian colleges such as Lynchburg Baptist College (now Liberty University), students could major in youth ministry. Denominational and interdenominational Christian publishing houses such as Youth Specialties and Group Publishing also launched youth ministry curriculum and youth meeting teaching materials.[6]

The following decade seemed to bring about a philosophical stability to the discipline of youth ministry. This stability was evidenced in the formation of organizations such as Sonlife Ministries by Dann Spader, whose vision was to establish a Great Commission emphasis in church youth groups.

"Perhaps the best known and most widely imitated church youth group in the nation during the 1980s was Son City (later called Student Impact), based in the Willow Creek Community Church. Each Tuesday evening 700-800 high school students made their way to the church located in South Barrington, Illinois, for competition, team activities and a powerful program which culminated in an evangelistic or pre-evangelistic message."[7]

The end of the twentieth century brought a renewed emphasis to reach out to public high school campuses.

The stirring event of the decade, of course, was the mass murders at Columbine High School in Littleton, Colorado, in the late '90s. This one event will long be remembered as a watershed experience that visualized the need for effective public school evangelism. Even though that on-campus violence staggered the nation, the Lord used the Christian testimonies of students Cassie Bernall and Rachel Scott as rallying cries for spiritual renewal across the country.

> Look at the history of youth ministry for inspiration and motivation.

I encourage all youth workers to look at the history of youth ministry for inspiration and motivation. You will notice that these visionary leaders saw specific needs in culture, and then they realized that those needs presented opportunities for effective ministry and outreach. Robert Raikes got up on Sunday mornings and took a walk through town. He saw needy children, and he envisioned meeting those needs by teaching them God's Word. Jack Wyrtzen and Percy Crawford noticed the growing youth culture following the Second World War, and they realized that young people could be reached for Christ through lively music and youth-oriented preaching. These are just two examples of why this study can be so encouraging. It demonstrates that youth today can also be reached with the gospel.

We can apply simple identifiable lessons to our

ministries with teenagers today. The first is that *effective youth outreach begins with a commitment to communicate the gospel.* Each of the ministries listed in this chapter began with a passion to share God's Word with young people. Their leaders worked hard to create and design relevant ways to present Biblical truth. The second lesson is that *each of these youth ministry examples saw clear cultural trends as opportunities for outreach.* Raikes saw kids with nothing to do; the early youth rallies welcomed the blossoming youth culture; Awana targeted youth's appetite for uniforms and badges; the on-campus clubs championed the desire for teenagers to spend quality time with their peers. The final lesson is that *visionary leaders established and organized significant ways of reaching youth with the gospel.* The people and organizations listed here are illustrations of how effective youth evangelism can be. These examples show how successful youth ministry organizations came into existence through the visionary and administrative skills of motivated leaders.

My purpose is not to endorse any of these organizations or approaches, but to say that I firmly believe that today's teenagers can be reached for Christ. It begins with a commitment to communicate the gospel. It demands someone who can identify current cultural trends as opportunities for evangelism, and it requires a vision of what can be accomplished and the administrative skills to make it happen. My burden is that this book will motivate local church youth workers to implement these three imperatives into the fabric of their ministries.

NOTES

1. Dean Borgman, "A History of American Youth Ministry," chap. 4 of *The Complete Book of Youth Ministry,* Warren S. Benson and Mark H. Senter III, eds. (Chicago: Moody Press, 1987), 61.

2. Benson and Senter, 69, 70.

3. Mark Senter III, *The Coming Revolution in Youth Ministry* (Wheaton, Ill.: Scripture Press Publications, Victor Books, 1992), 137.

4. Senter, 129–132.

5. Senter, 142.

6. Senter, 150.

7. Senter, 23.

CHAPTER 3

Developing Your Youth Evangelism Strategy

One of the major weaknesses of local church youth ministry is evangelism. Let's face it. Most churches are not doing a good job of teaching and training students to be effective in outreach. Churches tend to emphasize programs that minister to teenagers who are already part of their programs, but most of those who receive Christ will do so before age eighteen. Perhaps the church has allowed parachurch organizations to take the

> Perhaps the church has allowed parachurch organizations to take the lead in evangelistic outreach.

lead in evangelistic outreach. Ask yourself, Do these groups do a better job than we do in reaching students for Christ? It is time for local churches to develop a practical, well-defined, comprehensive strategy for evangelism.

> **Encourage and train students to share their faith with others.**

"Strategy" can be defined as a big-picture plan of action. I have met many youth workers who have led students to Christ, and I have talked to several high school students who are actively sharing their faith with others. I also know several youth workers who plan and host intermittent youth outreach events with varying degrees of success and effectiveness. I applaud these well-intentioned and highly motivated individuals for their desire to see people come to Christ and for their commitment to evangelism. However, too few churches have a comprehensive, big-picture strategy for youth evangelism.

Based upon my personal contact with several hundred youth workers over the past few years, I have developed four emphases to make youth evangelism an integral part of the church's overall youth ministry. I encourage pastors, youth pastors, and lay youth workers to implement all four suggestions into a comprehensive strategy for their youth ministries.

EMPHASIS 1: LIFESTYLE EVANGELISM

As with other matters, lifestyle evangelism can get out of balance. Some people think that lifestyle evangelism is the only way to witness; you cannot confront people with the gospel unless you know them well and have developed a personal and trusting relationship with them. Others contend that lifestyle evangelism is ineffective because it does not always utilize a verbal presentation the gospel.

I am not going to attempt to solve that issue here. Many books have already been written on the subject. My purpose is to encourage and train students to share their faith with others. That's why we must diligently train them to share their faith with friends, classmates, neighbors, relatives, and even strangers. This training must be a part of our equipping ministry with today's teenagers!

> Teenagers are likely to evangelize when classmates or friends ask about their beliefs.

Today's Christian students have regular opportunities to share their faith in Christ. I have found that lifestyle evangelism usually fits in one of three forms for high school students. First, teenagers are likely to evangelize when classmates or friends ask about their beliefs. First Peter 3:15 indicates this possibility: "Be ready always to give an answer to every man that asketh you a reason of the hope that is in you with meekness and fear."

Second, teenage believers will openly share the gospel when they have the occasion to work the plan of salvation into other conversations. Help your students visualize accounts, such as Christ's contact with the woman from Samaria in John 4. He naturally wove the gospel into His conversation. Some people are better at "conversational evangelism" than others. For instance, my wife has the God-given ability to turn almost every casual conversation (on airline flights, in grocery stores, at gas stations) into opportunities to share the gospel. That ability is not natural for me. Yet I have found that the Lord gives me many open doors to talk to people about Himself.

> Paul desired to make specific contacts for the expressed purpose of sharing the gospel.

The third way for students to share the gospel is by making appointments with others to talk about their faith. The account of the apostle Paul's defense before King Agrippa is recorded in Acts 26. An interesting principle, found near the end of that chapter, has great relevance. Verses 22 and 23 state that "I [Paul] continue unto this day, witnessing both to small and great, saying none other things than those which the prophets and Moses did say should come: That Christ should suffer, and that he should be the first that should rise from the dead, and should shew light unto the people." How motivating to think that Paul desired to make specific contacts for the expressed purpose of sharing the gospel.

Recently in my travels I have been thrilled to visit churches and youth groups where I have heard several testimonies of how God is using today's Christian students to share the gospel message with others. There certainly seems to be a renewed burden for evangelism, and I have been privileged to hear the stories of students taking or making specific opportunities to witness. However, these accounts of evangelism in action substantiate the need for youth workers to make sure their students are trained and prepared to share the gospel in these types of situations.

> Teach students at least one specific method of witnessing.

Here are some simple yet practical suggestions for training your teenagers to witness.

1. Teach your students a specific plan for witnessing. I firmly believe that most Christians (teens and adults) think they are inadequately prepared to share the gospel. That's why it is important to teach students at least one specific method of witnessing. I am not saying that there is only one way to witness. Certainly, that is not the case at all. However, confidence comes from knowing what to say and how to say it.

Many churches use the Roman's Road method effectively. Others use helps such as Evangelism Explosion, Contagious Christian, or God's Bridge to Eternal

Life.[1] Three different presentations of the gospel are also printed in the addendum of this book. Of course, many other outlines and organized plans are available. Study these various sources to determine which approach will work best for your group—or develop your own plan.

Again, let me emphasize that lifestyle evangelism begins with knowing how to share the gospel with others. It is not enough to live a good Christian life before a lost world. God expects every believer to share his or her faith. This statement does not mean that our students have to be polished and professional evangelists. However, we should do all we can to train students so that they know what to say when they come in contact with unsaved people.

I would be remiss not to add one other essential ingredient of sharing the gospel; that is, a person's individual testimony. Even a casual reading of the book of Acts reveals that the apostle Paul often shared his personal story as a way of telling others about Jesus Christ. The basic definition of a witness is someone who can verbalize what he or she has seen or heard. This idea is found in Acts 22:15, "For thou shalt be his witness unto all men of what thou hast seen and heard."

A person's testimony is powerful. It is a reality that no one can refute. Share with your students three basic aspects of a personal testimony: (1) what their life was like before they were saved; (2) how the Lord saved them; and (3) what their life is like since they have been saved. As a preparatory exercise in outreach training, ask your students to use this outline to write down their testimonies. It is easier for them to share their testimonies with others verbally after they have written them on paper.

> **Make sure your students know the Scriptures.**

2. Motivate your students to memorize verses and passages of Scripture to use with others. Make sure that your students know the Scriptures. Once you have determined which witnessing approach will work best with your students, lead your students in memorizing the appropriate passages. Never forget the truth of Romans 10:17: "Faith cometh by hearing, and hearing by the word of God." It's God's Word, not our outlines or methods, that changes people's lives. I encourage all youth workers to spend time in classroom situations and in one-on-one discipleship opportunities to make sure that their students know the Word of God. Real confidence in the ability to witness will come from confidence in the Scriptures.

3. Have resources available for your students to use. Provide gospel tracts, Bibles, and booklets for them to use on their own and to give to friends, classmates, and new converts. Place quality and relevant tracts and booklets in your youth room. When I was a youth pastor, one of the lay leaders in our church gave money so that our youth department always had extra Bibles available to give away to teenagers. Our church also provided pocket-size New Testaments for our students to use in their own witnessing endeavors. I believe it is important to have quality evangelistic resources available for your students and your adult workers.

4. *Give your students opportunities to practice giving the plan of salvation.* My experience has been that it is easier for students to give the gospel presentation outside of class if they have successfully gone over it a few times in positive and controlled classroom situations. Once you have trained your students in sharing one specific plan of salvation and encouraged them to memorize the corresponding Scripture passages, give them time to role-play sharing the gospel and Scripture with other students in your Sunday School or youth group. In fact, offer several opportunities to practice with multiple students. After they can confidently and successfully share their faith with others in class, they will be more likely to be confident and successful in situations outside of class.

5. *Develop a prayer list of specific unsaved people* (e.g., parents, friends, neighbors, coworkers). Prayer, of

course, is a significant part of any evangelistic effort for several specific reasons. First and foremost, prayer needs to be a priority because God answers prayer. Paul testified to the believers in Rome, "Brethren, my heart's desire and prayer to God for Israel is, that they might be saved" (Rom. 10:1). We should do all we can to encourage our students to follow Paul's example and pray specifically that unsaved people will come to Christ. Our students will truly rejoice when they see people for whom they have prayed come to accept Christ as their personal Savior.

> God uses prayer to put a personal burden on individuals' hearts for unsaved people.

The second reason for making prayer a major emphasis is that God uses prayer to put a personal burden on individuals' hearts for unsaved people. Consistent prayer for specific people will give students a burden for the people they are praying for. I know that God will use these prayers to give students opportunities to see people come to Christ. That's what makes it such a vital part of lifestyle evangelism. Prayer for unsaved people must be a top priority in youth ministry.

6. *Plan evangelistic events that will give your teens opportunities to invite their unsaved friends.* My experience has been that planning and hosting creative and quality evangelistic youth events is a fundamental part of any youth evangelistic strategy. Youth workers must do all

they can to train students so that they have the ability and the confidence to share the gospel with classmates, friends, and others on an individual basis. The next logical step in that process is for students to have events and activities to which they can invite unsaved friends. (See Emphasis 2 on page 41.) Sure, students should take the opportunities that God gives them to actively share their faith. But it is a natural part of teenage life to want to be with peers at quality youth events. Therefore, evangelistic events are important.

Evangelistic events are important.

7. *Preach and teach on the subject of evangelism to create an atmosphere of interest in outreach.* We must never forget that God's Word is the catalyst for spiritual growth. I don't believe that students, or anyone for that matter, will develop a burden for unsaved people without the Word of God. Evangelism must never be relegated to a program alone. It is not just a box that we can open and take out a bag of tricks. Evangelism is a spiritual exercise. It is God's business, but He expects us to be strong in our outreach endeavors for His glory. Only as we preach and teach from God's Word on the subject of evangelism will our students develop a spiritual emphasis on evangelism.

Implementing these suggestions will help train your students to share their faith on their own at school, at home, at work, or in other personal contacts with people.

EMPHASIS 2: EVENT EVANGELISM

The following statistic stresses the importance of including outreach events as specific opportunities for Christian students to invite their unsaved friends to hear the gospel: "Nine out of ten unchurched teens say they would go to church if they were invited by a friend."[2]

Because today's students are open to religion and spiritual things, I believe a key ingredient of local church ministry should be the development and planning of relevant and creative evangelistic events.

One only has to peruse a brief history of youth ministry (see chapter 2) to learn that the entire youth ministry movement has been characterized by a vast variety of youth outreach events. In the 1940s thousands of young people gathered in arenas such as Madison Square Garden to hear the gospel. Twenty years later, organizations such as Youth For Christ utilized outreach rallies and clubs to reach teens for Christ. In the 1980s Billy Graham and other evangelists hosted citywide crusades in an attempt to evangelize teenagers.

Other youth outreach methods actually morphed into megachurches as teens and their families came to Christ.[3] In this new millennium, students are again flocking to conferences, activities, and events that feature Christian music and strong Biblical preaching.

> Unsaved kids are likely to respond positively to invitations from people they trust.

On September 9, 2003, ABC News reported on *Good Morning America* that over 96 percent of American teenagers believe in God. A spiritual hunger exists among this country's youth. They are searching for truth, and they are open to hearing a holistic and comprehensive presentation of the gospel. Teenagers crave reality. They want to see genuine faith fleshed out in the lives of peers and trusted adults who care enough to be involved in the lives of students.

I believe, therefore, that unsaved kids are likely to respond positively to invitations from people they trust. That's why we need to train our students to share the gospel on their own, and why we need to organize and host events that our students will feel comfortable inviting their unsaved and unchurched friends to attend.

I see two distinct approaches in organizing youth outreach events. The first tactic is to design regular youth group meetings that are attractive and interesting to unsaved teenagers. The other is to schedule and plan relevant evangelistic events that will provide opportunities for your students to invite their unsaved friends to hear the gospel.

Designing youth group meetings to attract unsaved teens

This particular approach must begin with a clearly identified purpose of what you want to accomplish in your youth group meetings. Are you trying to help Christians grow in their faith, or are you attempting to reach unsaved kids for Christ? The purpose of your meetings should determine your program. If your objective is to make your regular meetings a time of outreach, you will need to structure the agenda of the meeting time so that it's applicable and inviting to unsaved, unchurched students.

> The purpose of your meetings should determine your program.

If reaching the unsaved is your purpose, then I encourage youth workers to start thinking like a visitor. This mind-set begins with **promotion.** How and where do you promote your meetings? You want unsaved teens to come; then why not post flyers or make announcements in public schools? You could also hang posters in other public places throughout your community where unsaved kids are likely to see them. Printing creative and professional flyers, handouts, posters, and other means of promotion for your students to use is essential. If outreach is your purpose, then the key is getting unsaved students to attend. Motivating them to come must be a primary aspect of your promotional efforts.

The second way to think like a visitor is to **program the meeting with unsaved teens in mind**. You'll probably have to ask yourself if your church is ready to structure your youth meetings in a way that will attract unsaved kids and motivate them to keep coming. I am not saying that effective outreach demands Scriptural compromise or worldly methodology. I do not endorse or believe in that kind of strategy. In fact, I have found that the methods you use to get kids to come in the first place are most likely the methods you will need to use to keep them coming. So if you resort to a fun-and-games mentality to attract them, you will probably need more fun and games to keep them. Youth workers, I urge you to be careful in adopting worldly methodology in an attempt at outreach. That being said, I do think that if you want your regular meetings to be open and inviting to unsaved kids, you will need to arrange your meeting times with unsaved and unchurched teens in mind. What this scenario looks like in your unique situation will obviously vary from church to church and from location to location. Just make sure that your meetings are relevant and interesting. Many educators are utilizing shorter presentation time periods and a variety of teaching methods.

In other words, do one activity for ten minutes, and then try an alternate activity for the next ten minutes, and so on.

Don't ever forget that the key to effective outreach is the clear, confident, and creative **presentation** of the Word of God. Sure, it's important to make positive first impressions, and it is imperative to build affirming relationships with community students. Those things are valid and beneficial steps toward outreach. However, we must remember that the Word of God

> It is imperative to build affirming relationships with community students.

is what changes people's lives (see Romans 10:17). Be certain that each meeting features a presentation of the gospel; then give students the opportunity to respond.

The final thing to consider is the importance of **people.** My own personal experience with teenagers tells me that teenagers attract other teenagers. This idea may seem obvious, but nonetheless the principle is true. Your regular church kids are unquestionably the main components in reaching other teens. I'm not just referring to a numbers thing, although there is something about that too. I don't think you will have many unchurched, unsaved community kids attending your youth group if they are all alone or if they are in the minority. It is threatening to be alone. So the youth program at your church must offer an atmosphere of warmth, energy, and excitement. And that starts with the regular members of your group.

Do they want unsaved visitors to attend? That question brings us to the obvious point: friendly people are attractive. You will need to train your group to be friendly. Your teens are probably like the adults in your church. We all tend to hang around with our friends, and we are insensitive to newcomers or visitors we do not know. You'll have to plan for friendliness, and ask the leaders in your group to model friendliness. As John 13:35 puts it, "By this shall all men know that ye are my disciples, if ye have love one to another."

> The youth program at your church must offer an atmosphere of warmth, energy, and excitement.

These four elements—promotion, program, presentation of the gospel, and people—are the main ingredients in making your church's regular youth meeting welcoming to unsaved guests.

I think that it is *possible* to develop an evangelistic atmosphere in your regular youth group meeting times that is welcoming, inviting, and maybe even contagious. As mentioned above, it is critically important for you to think through the purpose of those meetings and then develop your programming around that clearly defined purpose. Even though I have listed several important considerations to such an approach, I know that many churches are not adequately prepared to build their regularly scheduled youth meetings around outreach. Your church will need to commit the resources necessary to host weekly outreach meetings. That commitment will require administrative programming, budgeting, and qualified adult supervision. Those things take a great deal of work. In addition, the activities might take away an opportunity to use those meeting times as teaching or training occasions for your own young people. All I'm saying here is to think through what you are trying to do, then follow your strategy with quality and excellence.

> **follow your strategy with quality and excellence.**

Now I want to tell you about an interesting trend in youth evangelism that is certainly worthy of your prayerful consideration. In the last few months I have had the opportunity to witness some of the most amazing and effective outreach meetings in various locations around the country. The trend in many youth ministries is to move away from high-tech, multimedia programming in lieu of quieter, more relational and interpersonal approaches. Some use a coffeehouse approach, where the church creates a "Starbucks atmosphere" around small tables, quiet music, simple refreshments, and conversation. Others use a large, open room that gives kids a place to play simple board games and an opportunity to interact quietly with each other. It is interesting to me that this current trend of youth evangelism seems to be moving away from a glitzy, elaborate, and technologically savvy programming toward a more interpersonal and relationship-centered methodology.

> This current trend of youth evangelism seems to be moving away from a glitzy, elaborate, and technologically savvy programming.

Be sure to prayerfully think through the ramifications of this approach in your own church and ministry. Perhaps you should gear your weekly youth meetings toward evangelism, or maybe that strategy wouldn't be the best for your situation. I encourage all youth workers to examine the feasibility and practicality of a high-tech production versus a high-touch, interpersonal, relationship-building approach toward evangelism.

Planning special evangelistic events

The other approach is to schedule and plan creative and relevant events that provide special opportunities for your students to invite their unsaved friends to hear the gospel.

Most churches can host creative, periodic evangelistic youth events as an effective outreach in their communities. Christian youth should have the opportunity to invite their unsaved friends to events that use creative and relevant methods to present the gospel. Many churches cannot allocate the time or resources to do weekly evangelistic meetings, but those same churches can host some special evangelistic events each year. I have had the privilege of attending old-fashioned youth rallies, paintball wars, all-day bowling parties, "Capture the Flag" competitions, basketball tournaments, corn mazes, and a variety of other activities that churches have effectively used for evangelism.

> Sharing the plan of salvation is the purpose for hosting the event.

I contend that all outreach events for unsaved and unchurched teens should be distinguished by five essential characteristics.

First of all, *make sure that the gospel is clearly presented.* Sharing the plan of salvation is the purpose for hosting the event. I understand that times may arise when you would want to hold events with the sole purpose of developing relationships with community kids. Your goal is to share Christ with them at a later time. I'm sure that occasions may come when that strategy would be appropriate and even necessary.

I have also participated in church-sponsored youth events where the gospel presentation has had somewhat negative results. My own church hosted a Super Bowl party a couple of years ago that featured the game in a large-screen, projection format. Our church people provided free food for everyone, and our youth group worked hard to invite their unsaved friends from the community. We turned the game off at halftime while an excellent youth speaker shared the gospel. We found out later that some parents of the community teens were upset that we "shoved the Bible down the throats" of the kids. Undoubtedly that kind of reaction can happen. Preaching the Word of God can be an offense to unsaved people. My point is that, for the most part, when a church hosts an event, even unsaved, unchurched people expect some sort of "religious" presentation. More importantly, it is the Word of God that changes people's lives and brings them to salvation. So it is certainly worth that risk to creatively yet confidently present the gospel during youth outreach events. Present it in various ways, utilizing an assortment of creative methods—from preaching to tract distribution.

> It is the Word of God that changes people's lives and brings them to salvation.

Second, I encourage youth workers to *make sure that the gospel presentation is a priority* during the event's activities. This point sounds much like my first one, but here is an example. Several years ago I accepted an invitation to fly to the Midwest and speak at a large evangelistic youth outreach. The group that asked me to speak took care of my flight, put me up in a nice hotel, paid for a rental car, and even gave me a generous honorarium. The leaders of the event also asked me to make sure that I presented the gospel during my message. I arrived at the event and found several hundred teenagers participating in a creative and well-planned activity. The event's organizers had previously told the kids that the activity would be finished by 10:30 that evening. The event's activities took a lot longer than expected and after introducing me to speak at 10:26, the person in charge whispered to me, "Mel, I'm sorry, but you have to quit on time." They paid for my flight, my hotel, a rental car, and gave me an honorarium, but they gave me only four minutes to speak and to share the gospel. Youth workers, this situation ought not to be. Please plan ahead and leave plenty of time for the presentation of the gospel.

> **Leave plenty of time for the presentation of the gospel.**

The third characteristic of effective outreach events is to *follow up on those who attend.* Your goals are to see teens come to Christ, grow in Christ, and ultimately become functioning participants in your church and youth group. These goals will undoubtedly require an organized plan to follow up on those who attend an outreach event. You could begin by giving your visitors some sort of "guest packet" that gives them more information about your group's regular meetings and activities. Make sure the guests fully understand that they are welcome to attend your regular youth meetings or activities. Please do not assume that the visitors will naturally feel that they are welcome to keep attending. (Remember my advice: we must learn to think like visitors ourselves to help us understand what they are going through.) You could also follow up on visitors by calling them on the phone, sending them e-mails, or by visiting in their homes. This strategy necessitates a way of obtaining personal information from each guest. Probably the best way of gaining information is to have all of the teenagers who attend (regular church kids and visitors) fill out some sort of registration card for the activity. The goal is to make your guests feel welcome at your events and then to invite them to future events.

> **Make sure the guests fully understand that they are welcome to attend your regular youth meetings or activities.**

Perhaps the best way to follow up with teenagers after outreach events is to try to assimilate them into a small group ministry. It is much less threatening for guests and new students to be involved in a small group of six to eight students than it is for them in the entire youth group. A small group ministry allows students to develop stronger and deeper interpersonal relationships. That approach is mutually beneficial to the new students (helps them form relationships) and to the regular members of your youth group (helps them reach out to visitors).

Fourth, make sure you *organize and execute your outreach events with quality and professionalism.* Think like a teenager for a moment. Would you want to invite your unsaved friends to an event that was poorly organized or an embarrassment to you? Most likely you would not invite unsaved people to something that was not a top quality, professional event. So do your best to make sure that your evangelistic events reflect excellence.

> **A small group ministry allows students to develop stronger and deeper interpersonal relationships.**

Planning is fundamental for any successful event. Details are extremely important. The event should start on time and end on time. Arrange to have plenty of adult leaders. If you do not have administrative skills, recruit someone else from your youth staff or church membership to assist you in planning your outreach events. Let's face it, quality events are a reflection on your church and a good testimony for the Lord.

The fifth characteristic that I want to mention is to *plan interesting, relevant, and creative events.* Consider surveying your regular students to determine what events would work for an evangelistic outreach. In some communities paintball works well. Other communities respond positively to basketball tournaments. Let me give you a piece of advice on this subject. Just because something worked well as an outreach when you were a kid doesn't mean it will necessarily work well now. Please think through what you are trying to do. Be creative instead of just going with something "old hat." Make sure that your outreach events are interesting to students and relevant for today's youth culture.

> **Make sure that your outreach events are interesting to students and relevant for today's culture.**

Evidence substantiates the claim that evangelistic youth events are still quite successful and profitable. Perhaps as never before, today's teens are gathering at major youth ministry events across the country and around the world. It has probably always been true that teens attract other teens.

EMPHASIS 3: PUBLIC SCHOOL OUTREACH

According to *The World Almanac and Book of Facts 2004*, almost fifty million young people attend America's public schools. And according to the birth rate, that number will increase significantly during the next several years. This "mission field" is huge. Compare it to twenty million total people in Australia, thirty-one million people in Canada, and twenty-seven million people in Peru.[4] Get the point? America's public schools form a larger mission field than the entire population of several other countries.

What can you do to reach out to the unsaved students attending the high schools in your community? "Separation of church and state" issues have impacted our strategy and methodology. Many of these stories have come from secular as well as religious news sources. Some schools do not allow prayer or religious influence during graduation or other school-sponsored activities. Others do not allow local church youth pastors on their campuses. They allow students to gather in prayer groups or Bible studies.

Yet people are sharing amazing stories of how God is working in public schools across our nation. Events such as the previously mentioned See You at the Pole have recorded ever-growing numbers of teenagers involved in outreach.

According to *Group* Magazine,

> The Department of Education has issued new guidelines for students' religious expression on campus that give them greater freedom to express their beliefs. Officials now say students can
> • Communicate their religious beliefs in class assignments.

- Pray and read their Bibles or other religious resources during non-instructional times "to the same extent that they may engage in nonreligious activities."
- Organize prayer meetings and Bible or religious clubs before or after school hours to the same extent other extracurricular activities are allowed.
- Speak about their religious beliefs at assemblies, as long as they were selected on a neutral basis (school officials can also issue disclaimers that the school does not endorse the student's views).

School districts will be barred from receiving federal education funds unless they certify they have no policies limiting constitutionally protected religious expression.[5]

Plan creative ways of outreach in public schools in your community.

Youth worker, I encourage you to plan creative ways of outreach in public schools in your community. Of course, the best methods of outreach will be led and initiated by students, but another effective way for you to be involved in public schools is by volunteering to help. Probably every public school district in this country is looking for assistance from caring adult volunteers. You may have athletic abilities or musical talents and could volunteer to help with a sports or music program. You may be able to substitute teach. If you have a commercial driver's license (CDL), you may want to consider driving a school bus. Many schools also need adult chaperones for field trips or other student activities. Be patient. Your particular school may not be open toward you the first time you try, but keep trying.

Be persistent. Look for ways to reach out in America's public schools.

Our church (along with sister churches in our community) has successfully opened the door via a "released time" program of religious instruction. The state of Pennsylvania, for instance, still allows religious instruction for public school students. Our church hosts a Protestant released time program one morning or afternoon each month in our church building. We have to provide transportation, and the students must obtain written parental permission prior to leaving the school property. We also turn in a general outline of our curriculum, including choices of topics and speakers. But we have found that our school district is open and willing to accommodate us in this joint venture with other Bible-believing churches.

> Look for ways to reach out in America's public schools.

The following suggestions may help you determine a course of action for outreach into the public schools in your area.

1. Make an appointment with the school administrator to see if the school will allow you to hold a Bible study, Bible club, or prayer group in school facilities. The school may not allow outside adults to participate, but due to "equal access" laws passed by the U.S. Supreme Court, the school should allow students to hold such groups.[6]

2. Obtain a copy of the school calendar and plan out-

reach events around popular school activities. Consider activities such as homecoming, prom, and football games. For example, one youth worker told me that his church hosts a tailgate party in the parking lot of the high school's football stadium before each home football game as an outreach opportunity.

3. *Hold a Bible study or prayer group in an off-campus location near the school.* Survey your youth group to determine the best time and location. Public high schools may not want Bible studies on campus, but with a little bit of thought and creativity, you should be able to secure an off-campus site nearby.

4. *Have your teens obtain permission to post flyers or posters in the school building announcing your outreach events.* Most schools allow student-oriented groups to hang flyers or posters in designated spots on campus.

5. *Teach your teens to share their faith in Christ at school.* Don't forget to train and motivate your students to take every opportunity the Lord gives them to share their faith at school.

6. *Ask God for a committed Christian teacher in your school system who is willing to serve as an advisor for a Bible club on campus* (patterned after programs such as Fellowship of Christian Athletes or Campus Life).

Developing Your Youth Evangelism Strategy

7. *Contact parachurch agencies for ideas and methods.* You may not be able to endorse all of their theology or methods, but they often have worthwhile ideas and suggestions.

8. *Encourage interested adults in your church to volunteer for athletic programs, drama, music, and field trips.* Public schools are often looking for adult volunteers for their various programs due to budget cutbacks and other needs. Other adults may consider running for the school board or serving on the adult education committee, the parents' advisory committees, the PTA, and other administrative roles. If you volunteer your time at a local school, make sure that you are faithful and dependable at what you committed to do there. Your testimony is at stake.

> Be creative and persistent as you attempt to reach this important mission field.

These ideas are merely suggestions. The local church can do many other things to have an effective outreach in its community's public schools. Be creative and persistent as you attempt to reach this important mission field.

EMPHASIS 4:
DOOR-TO-DOOR OR VISITATION OUTREACH

I understand that some church growth experts claim that door-to-door or visitation evangelism is outdated in today's culture. They quote community regulations that prohibit soliciting and other cultural barriers. In addition, certain religious cults have caused damage because of their overly zealous reputations in some areas of the country. However, I am convinced that many creative ways to utilize door-to-door or visitation evangelism still exist. This methodology can give students opportunities to share their faith, and it can also promote church activities or functions.

> **Many creative ways to utilize door-to-door evangelism still exist.**

A few years ago I learned that a leading evangelical college took a survey of several thousand Christian teenagers. Along with several other questions, the survey asked the teens about their involvement in evangelism. One particular question stood out: "Do you witness enough?" Over 99 percent of the teens answered no. A follow-up question asked the teens to list reasons for that negative answer. Three excuses were identified: (1) "I don't know how"; (2) "I don't know anybody who is unsaved"; (3) "No one else is doing it."

If these three reasons are still valid, then an effective youth outreach program would seek to eliminate the negative responses.

1. "I don't know how."

Take every opportunity to teach and train your young people how to share the gospel. Perhaps you could use the Romans Road, the Bridge illustration, or maybe even an established outline such as the one provided by Evangelism Explosion. (See Emphasis 1 on page 32.)

Students will not share the gospel if they don't know what to say. Also, accountability is involved if all your students are learning the same basic outline of the gospel. Teens are peer oriented. By teaching one specific way of witnessing, your students are more likely to develop a positive peer pressure toward it. Adult youth workers must make sure that they model their own knowledge of the outline before they try to encourage the students to learn it. I think it is also wise to recruit a small team of spiritual leaders in the group to start doing what you are asking the other students to do. Then give these students some public exposure to the rest of the group. Give them opportunities to share their evangelistic endeavors with their peers. The final step is to encourage other students to make learning this gospel presentation a priority.

> Students will not share the gospel if they don't know what to say.

2. *"I don't know anybody who is unsaved."*

Statistically it is true that the longer someone has been saved, the fewer unsaved friends a person will have. This area is where a visitation ministry can be utilized effectively. Many ideas can be implemented successfully in a local church setting. Teenagers can distribute flyers or tracts door-to-door (some communities may require a permit); take a survey on religion at a local shopping center (obtain permission from the owner if the center is private property); visit regular attendees of church or youth group to encourage them; follow up visitors or inactive kids; visit nursing homes, hospitals, or contacts made during evangelistic events.

> The longer someone has been saved, the fewer unsaved friends a person will have.

3. *"No one else is doing it."*

Several ideas may help motivate your group to share their faith. Establish a set time for visitation, possibly one night per week or a specific day for a visitation blitz. Determine which time schedule works best for your group. Promote your outreach events in every way possible. Get commitments from your key teens. Use accountability as effective peer pressure.

One church that I visited sets aside a Saturday afternoon each quarter for a specific visitation evangelistic outreach. Each outreach day has a time of prayer and training on methods the teens will use. The training includes motivation and an opportunity to role-play various situations the teens may encounter. The youth leaders then go with the teens to the outreach locations (e.g., door-to-door, downtown, survey sites, hospitals) in their community to distribute gospel tracts or promotional materials about their church or

Developing Your Youth Evangelism Strategy

specific church ministries such as Vacation Bible School. I observed that this church's approach to visitation solves each of the three objections listed above. (1) The leaders train the students in what they were asking them to do. (2) The community contacts puts the teens in touch with unsaved, unchurched people. (3) By organizing scheduled times for outreach, more students are able to participate.

This particular church situation provides an illustration of three important principles for visitation outreach. First, there is strength in numbers. I have found it much easier to motivate teenagers for evangelism if other teens are going to be involved as well. You may have to start this process by recruiting individual students instead of making a mass appeal. Prayer will be an important part of this recruiting process. You should pray specifically that the Lord will put a burden on the hearts of some of your students to be actively involved in outreach. Second, by scheduling a visitation event only once per quarter, the students will not get burned out or tired of that method. Third, visitation provides a way for almost anyone to be involved in outreach. Young people can be trained easily to hand out flyers or other promotional items. This approach

> It's much easier to motivate teenagers for evangelism if other teens are going to be involved as well.

does not require sophisticated training, yet it provides significant opportunities to briefly share the gospel and to be a good testimony for Christ in the community.

I want to tell you about another visitation idea that is used effectively across the country: gift distribution. I originally heard about this approach from a friend who is a youth pastor in Indiana. His youth group annually schedules a 9-volt battery giveaway. He encourages his entire youth group to show up at the church before dispersing into community neighborhoods to give away free batteries for people's smoke detectors. The church finds companies that are willing to provide the batteries at a reasonable cost. This particular giveaway is easier than the youth pastor expected because of community awareness of fire departments and safety-related issues. This church's leaders are convinced that the 9-volt battery giveaway is an effective way of showing the community that their people care.

> **Young people can be trained easily to hand out flyers or other promotional items.**

Other churches are involved in similar ministries. The principle is that going door-to-door can be quite effective if you are willing to provide a service for the community.

Let's not ignore visitation as an important method

in our desire to develop a local church youth evangelism strategy. These four areas of emphasis—lifestyle evangelism, event evangelism, public school outreach, and visitation or door-to-door outreach—can combine to form a big-picture, comprehensive strategy for churches that want to make youth evangelism a top priority.

NOTES

1. See www.youthee.org, www.contagiouschristian.com, or www.majestic-media.com.

2. See www.barna.org/cgi-bin/PageCategory.asp?CategoryID=37.

3. Lynne Hybels and Bill Hybels, *Rediscovering Church: The Story and Vision of Willow Creek Community Church* (Grand Rapids: Zondervan Publishing House, 1995), 29-33.

4. *The World Almanac and Book of Facts 2004* (New York: World Almanac Education Group, Inc., 2004), 219, 855, 856.

5. "Trendwatch: Christian Expression on Campus," *Group* Magazine (May-June 2003). For the full list of guidelines, go to the Department of Education's Web site at www.ed.gov.

6. See www4.law.cornell.edu/uscode/20/4071.html for the full legal wording on the equal access ruling.

CHAPTER 4

Outreach Ideas

I gleaned the following list of youth outreach ideas from a survey I took of four hundred youth workers. The volunteer youth workers and vocational youth pastors who took my survey represented both small and large churches. Some of the respondents were veteran youth workers, while others were newcomers to youth ministry.

You will notice that some of these ideas require a great deal of planning and administration; others can be accomplished quite easily. Please remember that the cause of Christ deserves careful planning and quality work. The testimony of our church and youth ministry may be at stake. It is also worth noting, once again, that the purpose is evangelism, not just promo-

> **The cause of Christ deserves careful planning and quality work.**

tion. I believe with all my heart that these projects can be feasible vehicles to share the gospel with those who need Christ.

I also must remind you that your teenagers can witness to people from all age groups—not just other teenagers. Don't be reluctant to design evangelistic endeavors to reach out to children and then do something else geared to teenagers. Teenagers can be used to reach adults for Christ as well. Make sure that your students know their audience. Your training should clearly identify the specific group of people your group is targeting.

> **My prayer is that these ideas will whet your appetite for other events or opportunities.**

I encourage you to read through this list with an open mind. Ask yourself these questions: What can I do in my situation? What specific ideas would be effective in my community? What resources are available to me? How can I creatively utilize these resources for evangelism?

My prayer is that these ideas will whet your appetite for other events or opportunities. For instance, you may not have the facilities or expertise to host an evangelistic sports clinic, but your group could write and produce your own gospel tract. You may not have any students who can write for the local newspaper, but you might have a student who could design an evangelistic Web site. Be creative and dream a little bit, but be sure to pray. Only God knows what things are possible in your community.

Random Acts of Kindness. Hand out gifts (e.g., ice-cold sodas on a hot day) at a high-traffic area, such as a gas station, a rest stop, or the airport; do not take money; give out gospel tracts and church literature.

Community Work Projects. Work for free (e.g., host a free car wash; rake leaves; clean a local park or highway); give out gospel tracts and church literature.

Write Your Own Tract. Involve young people who have writing and desktop publishing experience or interest; write and edit tract; include youth group testimonies; print the tract (best quality possible); distribute it.

Newspaper Outreach. Find a student with writing interest or experience; ask him or her to write a youth column for a local paper; follow the paper's guidelines; share information about your church or current issues.

Youth Group Web Site. Involve your young people; list youth group and church activities and schedules; add photos of kids; include the gospel and a response device for follow-up; promote the site.

Sports Clinic. Host a sports clinic; involve your athletes; invite local children's teams; get permission to host the clinic at an appropriate location (e.g., a soccer field, a gymnasium, a baseball diamond, or your church facilities); obtain qualified coaches and instructors; develop a plan to present the gospel.

Youth Choir or Band. Organize a youth group ensemble or band; provide quality leadership; practice and learn the music; get permission to sing in a public place (e.g., a mall, nursing homes); develop a plan to share the gospel.

Travel Teams. Assemble a ministry team (e.g., music, drama, puppets) and take your team on the road; find public places to host your team (ask permission first); develop a creative way to share the gospel and/or distribute church literature.

Media Projects. Encourage your students to produce a media presentation (e.g., film, video, slides, Internet, PowerPoint); find an outlet for the production; present the gospel in the production or afterwards.

Puppet Team. Secure quality puppets, stage, scripts, music; provide training for group; practice, practice, practice; perform the production in a public place (e.g., a park, a mall, child care locations); provide quality leadership; present the gospel during or following the production.

Backyard Bible Clubs. Secure locations in the community (parks or someone's backyard); train your students to teach the lesson, play games, control the children, teach memory verses, lead Bible learning activities, tell missions stories, and make crafts; practice ahead of time; clearly present the gospel.

Visitation. Go door-to-door in your community to

hand out tracts, Bibles, or church literature; check community solicitation laws; visit newcomers or visitors of church, Sunday School, or youth group; follow common sense safety rules (e.g., go in pairs).

Public School Bible Clubs. Encourage students who attend public school to start an on-campus group; check out what other student organizations are allowed to meet on campus and the regulations those groups must meet (e.g., your students may need to identify a Christian teacher or advisor for their group). Some schools are open; in other schools the students may need to be more creative in trying to reach their peers for Christ. Resources are available from several sources.

Off-campus Bible Club or Prayer Group. Locate a place for a student group to meet somewhere near the school for before-school or after-school functions; possibilities include a restaurant or other public building, the home of a church member, or the church building itself.

See You at the Pole. Encourage your students to pray at the school flagpole the third Wednesday in September; train students how to share their faith afterwards; pray much. (See chapter 1 for additional information on this event.)

Community Outreach. Plan and host a community event (e.g., a holiday outreach; a prayer breakfast for community officials; a block party); obtain permission from community authorities; schedule around other holiday activities; train students for specific projects (e.g., music; games; fair booth); share church information and the gospel, if possible.

Evangelistic Events. Host a concert or other evangelistic event; check into renting the high school auditorium or a gymnasium for this purpose; promote it widely; encourage your kids to invite their unsaved friends; present the gospel in a creative and effective manner; be ready to offer counseling for needy teens; follow up on those who attend.

Nursing Homes or Hospitals. Take your students to visit people in a nursing home or hospital; present a service or visit each room; give small gifts to the residents or patients; be sensitive to the staff; distribute gospel literature and church information.

Youth or Juvenile Home. Arrange to visit with residents one-on-one or as a group; give gifts or gospel tracts; follow the home's guidelines and policies.

Parent-of-Teens Seminar. Invite unsaved parents of teenagers or preteens to a seminar at your church or at a neutral location; publicize it in every way possible; invite qualified speakers; make it a quality event; do not be afraid to share Biblical principles; share church information; plan to follow up on those who attend.

Fifth Quarter Event. Hold an evangelistic event at your church (or at some other central location) immediately following the high school football or basketball games; brainstorm to determine appropriate activities; offer food and beverages; present the gospel; follow up on those who attend.

Tailgate Parties at High School Football Games. Set up a grill and cook hot dogs (or whatever your budget can afford); offer the food at no charge to high school kids (you'll have a crowd!); present the gospel or church information; use music to attract attention to your site.

Open Gym Nights. Open your church's gymnasium or rent the public school gym; invite kids to come and play basketball or volleyball; make stipulations (e.g., in order to play basketball, you have to stay for the Bible study); offer adequate adult supervision; check on insurance; follow up on those who attend.

Public Park Outreach. Present a children's club in a public park; bring sports equipment and offer recreation; present the gospel and church literature; provide adequate adult supervision.

Youth Centers. Build or secure a "hang-out" place for kids (café; coffeehouse); plan activities for students; provide adequate adult supervision; check on safety and legal issues.

Other Ideas. This list only scratches the surface. What could you do? What else could be done in your community to reach people for Christ and to train your kids to develop a lifestyle of evangelism?

Conclusion

Greg Stier presents three advantages of evangelizing the Millennial Generation in his book titled *Outbreak: Creating a Contagious Youth Ministry through Viral Evangelism*.

His first "advantage" is that students today are "more experiential than logical." They "feel more than they think. How is that an advantage? Easy! Christianity is both experiential and logical. We have the tools to capture both the mind and the heart of the typical teenager today."[1]

This bent toward experience gives us a huge advantage in sharing the gospel. Whereas past generations wanted arguments, this generation is open to the life-changing and heart-changing events in which the truth of the gospel is clearly and creatively presented. God may be giving us an open door to host evangelistic events that can and will attract unsaved kids. Today's students are open to that kind of strategy; they may be more willing to participate in those kinds of event than ever before.

Stier's second "advantage" is that students today are "more open to talking about spiritual things."[2]

As I have previously emphasized, religion is a big deal in today's society. Religious books are best sellers; WWJD bracelets are a national fashion symbol; and Christian music is a multibillion-dollar industry. Yes, young people today are open to religion and religious things. This openness gives your Christian students unparalleled opportunities to share their faith with others. We must work hard, therefore, to ensure that our students know how to share the gospel with their friends, coworkers, family members, neighbors, and classmates. Accountability comes with teaching your students a specific approach or outline for witnessing. Whatever method you choose, make sure your students know how to share the good news of Jesus Christ with confidence and clarity. They will have many opportunities to share it.

Stier's third "advantage" is that "teenagers love a good story. . . . Christianity is the greatest story ever told! We need to learn how to tell it in all of its fascinating glory. Like a great novel, it is full of twists and turns and intrigue. But unlike a novel, it is not fiction. It is a love story that just happens to be true."[3]

Students also love to hear the stories of what has happened in someone else's life. That's why the Regular Baptist Press student ministries curriculum often encourages Sunday School teachers to invite adults and other church people to the youth class to share testimonies of what God has done in their lives. There is something special about a personal testimony or story. It's true. It actually happened to someone— and students respond to that.

At Regular Baptist Press, we use our student publications to tell the stories of real-life kids with real-life stories of what God is doing. It's amazing to see kids respond to these stories. Wise youth workers will be sure to tap in to the power of a testimony in their own situations as well.

We live in a culture that gives our students tremendous opportunities to share the gospel. Therefore, we must teach them how to share their testimonies with others. May the Lord bless you as you train and encourage your group to share their faith!

Notes

1. Greg Stier, *Outbreak: Creating a Contagious Youth Ministry through Viral Evangelism* (Chicago: Moody Press, 2002), 188.

2. Stier, 190.

3. Stier, 191.

ADDENDUM

Gospel Presentations

THE ROMAN'S ROAD TO SALVATION

Everyone is a sinner.

Romans 3:10, 11—"As it is written, There is none righteous, no, not one: There is none that understandeth, there is none that seeketh after God."

Romans 3:23—"For all have sinned, and come short of the glory of God."

The penalty for sin is death, but Christ has already paid that price.

Romans 6:23—"For the wages of sin is death; but the gift of God is eternal life through Jesus Christ our Lord."

God loved us enough to send His Son to die for us.

Romans 5:8—"But God commendeth his love toward us, in that, while we were yet sinners, Christ died for us."

We must accept God's gift of salvation by faith.

Romans 10:9, 10—"That if thou shalt confess with thy mouth the Lord Jesus, and shalt believe in thine heart that God hath raised him from the dead, thou shalt be saved. For with the heart man believeth unto righteousness; and with the mouth confession is made unto salvation."

You can know for sure that you have eternal life.

1 John 5:13—"These things have I written unto you that believe on the name of the Son of God; that ye may know that ye have eternal life, and that ye may believe on the name of the Son of God."

God's Bridge to Eternal Life[1]

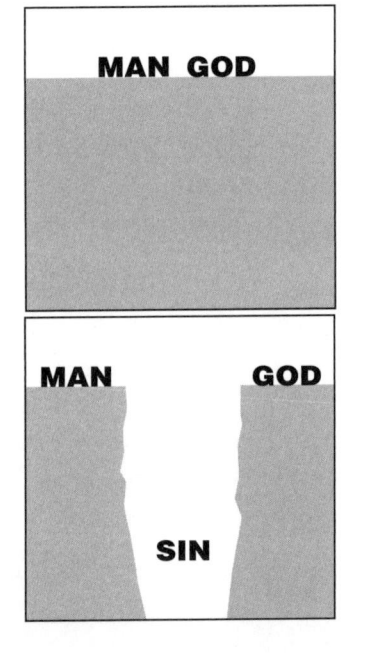

1. The Plan

God loves you and created you to have a personal relationship with Him.

Colossians 1:16—"All things were created by him, and for him."

2. The Gap

Our sin keeps us from having a personal relationship with God.

Romans 3:23—"For all have sinned, and come short of the glory of God."

Addendum—Gospel Presentations

3. The Bridge
Only through Jesus Christ can you have a personal relationship with God.

John 14:6—"Jesus saith unto him, I am the way, the truth, and the life: no man cometh unto the Father, but by me."

4. The Action
You must personally respond by trusting Jesus as Savior.

John 3:16—"For God so loved the world, that he gave his only begotten Son, that whosoever believeth in him should not perish, but have everlasting life."

THE ROMANS 6:23 BRIDGE[2]

"For the wages of sin is death; but the gift of God is eternal life through Jesus Christ our Lord."

"For the (wages) of (sin) is (death;) but the (gift) of (God) is (eternal life) (through Jesus Christ) our Lord."

Ask the student to read aloud the verse in the box. Explain the separation that exists between God and us (people) because of sin and death. Instruct him or her to circle the words "wages," "sin," and "death." Direct the student to write each key word ("wages," "sin," and

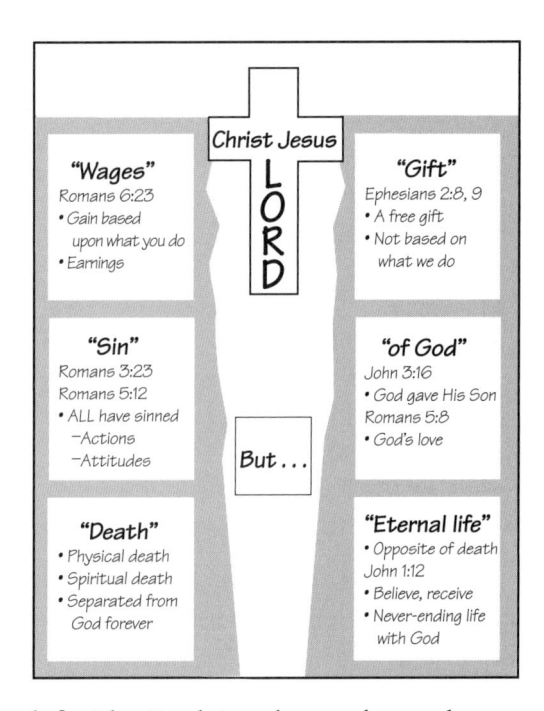

	Christ Jesus L O R D	
"Wages" Romans 6:23 • Gain based upon what you do • Earnings		**"Gift"** Ephesians 2:8, 9 • A free gift • Not based on what we do
"Sin" Romans 3:23 Romans 5:12 • ALL have sinned —Actions —Attitudes	But …	**"of God"** John 3:16 • God gave His Son Romans 5:8 • God's love
"Death" • Physical death • Spiritual death • Separated from God forever		**"Eternal life"** • Opposite of death John 1:12 • Believe, receive • Never-ending life with God

"death") on the left side. Explain what each word means. Ask the student to circle the words "gift," "of God," and "eternal life," and to underline "our Lord." Then have him or her write the key words on the right. Again, explain what each word means. Tell how God has provided the free gift of eternal life. State that each of us has sinned and deserves to be separated from God forever, but God has given us the gift of eternal life. Have the person write "but" in the bottom box. Draw a cross. Write the words "Christ Jesus" on the cross and explain how Jesus Christ is our bridge to "eternal life." Then write in "Lord" and explain that Christ wants and deserves to be the Lord of our life. Give the student the opportunity to accept Christ's free gift by faith in Him.

NOTES

1. This salvation presentation is adapted from a tract titled "God's Bridge to Eternal Life," published by Majestic Media, 52244 D W Seaton, Chesterfield, MI 48047.

2. I learned this presentation of the gospel from Bryan Waggoner, who directs student ministries at Bethesda Baptist Church of Brownsburg, Indiana.

Selected Bibliography

Barna, George. *Real Teens.* Ventura, Calif.: Regal Books, 2001.

Benson, Warren S., and Mark H. Senter III, eds. *The Complete Book of Youth Ministry.* Chicago; Moody Press, 1997.

Howe, Neil, and William Strauss. *Millennials Go to College.* Great Falls, Va.: American Association of Collegiate Registrars, 2003.

Howe, Neil, and William Strauss. *Millennials Rising: The Next Great Generation.* New York: Random House, Vintage Books, 2000.

Hybels, Lynne, and Bill Hybels. *Rediscovering Church: The Story and Vision of Willow Creek Community Church.* Grand Rapids: Zondervan Publishing House, 1995.

McAllister, Dawson. *Saving the Millennial Generation.* Nashville: Thomas Nelson Publishers, 1999.

Rahn, Dave, and Terry Linhart. *Contagious Faith: Empowering Student Leadership in Youth Evangelism.* Loveland, Colo.: Group Publishing, 2000.

Rainer, Thom S. *The Bridger Generation.* Nashville: Broadman & Holman Publishers, 1997.

Senter III, Mark. *The Coming Revolution in Youth Ministry.* Wheaton, Ill.: Scripture Press Publications, Victor Books, 1992.

St. Clair, Barry. *The Magnet Effect.* Stone Mountain, Ga.: Reach Out Youth Solutions, 1994.

St. Clair, Barry, and Keith Naylor. *Penetrating the Campus: Reaching Kids Where They Are.* Stone Mountain, Ga.: Reach Out Youth Solutions, 2002.

Stier, Greg. Outbreak: *Creating a Contagious Youth Ministry through Viral Evangelism.* Chicago: Moody Press, 2002.

Veerman, David R. *Youth Evangelism: Building Bridges to Touch Young Lives.* Wheaton, Ill.: Scripture Press Publications, Victor Books, 1996.